How to Draw

Fashion Figures

In Simple Steps

First published in Great Britain 2012

Search Press Limited
Wellwood, North Farm Road,
Tunbridge Wells, Kent TN2 3DR

Reprinted 2013, 2014

ISBN: 978 1 84448 764 6

Printed in Malaysia

Dedication

*In memory of my
beloved Mum.*

How to Draw

Fashion Figures

In Simple Steps

Susie Hodge

Search Press

Introduction

Fashion designers and illustrators have always communicated their ideas through their drawings, which although personal, have widespread appeal. Fashion illustration is greatly admired and enjoyed for its own sake. Elongation and simplification are two of the main methods used for fashion figure drawing, and the best fashion illustrations are created with a blend of reality and fantasy.

This book will help you draw your own fashion figures, showing you the simple stages involved. Every figure is built up in sequential stages – words are not needed. All you have to do is to follow each stage carefully and finish off the image as you prefer. There are twenty-eight illustrations, each set out in a similar way: in the first step, simple purple lines show you how to mark on the most basic underlying structure of the figure. In the next step, the previous purple lines are green, and new lines are added in purple, showing how to start to 'flesh out' your figure. In the third step, the previous purple lines have become green, and new purple lines show how to begin to place such elements as hands, hair, shoes, facial features and some clothes. In stage four, preceding purple marks are green and new purple lines build up details such as facial features, hair, clothing, accessories and some shading. The fifth image on each page is completed in pencil and the sixth and final image is a watercolour version of the illustration, to show you an option of what you could do.

When you are following each stage, use a sharp HB, B or 2B pencil. Draw lightly so that any initial unwanted lines can be erased easily. Your final work could be in pencil, pen, coloured pencils, felt tips, watercolour or acrylics – or even collage, depending on how confident you feel and the look you are going for.

I hope you will draw all the figures in this book. Once you have gained confidence, draw further fashion figures using the simple construction method I have shown. Elongation and simplification are important, but also remember that the figures are three-dimensional and clothing wraps around them, so try to visualise this, as well as textures. Whether you are working towards a career in this area or are drawing the figures for pure pleasure, I hope you have fun and soon develop your own unique style.

Happy Drawing!

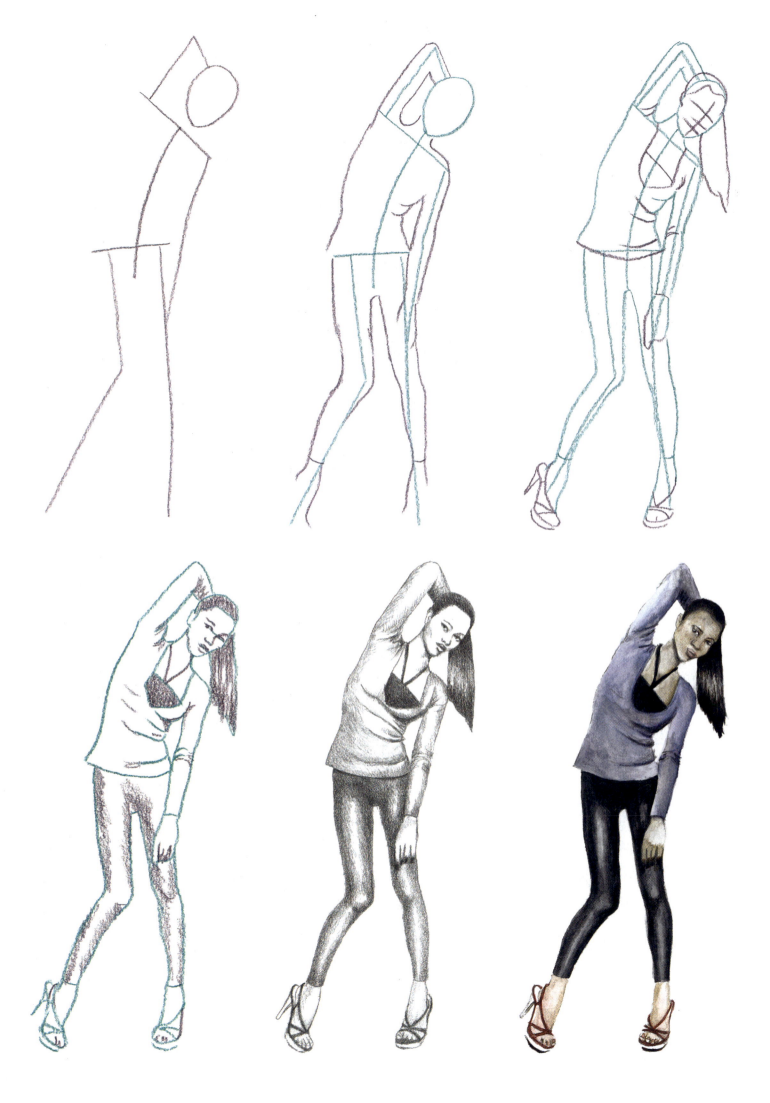